STAINED GLASS SUNCATCHER PATTERNS

YOU CAN ALSO SELL

~ Francis Elder II

STAINED GLASS SUNCATCHER PATTERNS

YOU CAN ALSO SELL

© Francis Elder II - Creations By Elder
PO Box 782 Kansas, OK 74347
frank@creationsbyelder.com
WHOLESALE INQUIRES WELCOMED

1st Edition August 2017

My name is Francis Elder II and my voyage into stained glass began back in 1988 while I was still in high school in Siloam Springs, Arkansas. I always liked to take art and you could find me doodling on a piece of scrap paper at any given moment in time.

Our shop trades teacher Louie knew this and asked me if I would like to help with a project he wanted to do for V.I.C.A. (Vocational Industrial Clubs of America), which turned out to be a set of three stained glass panels. I thought this would be a lot of fun and said yes.

From there I helped with the drawing of the design, then the full sized pattern and then contributed my time to help actually produce the panels. A wonderful lady by the name of Beatrice Stebbing who owned a stained glass studio in town donated her expertise, time and materials to help accomplish this project. She was one of the kindest and most inspiring people I had met.

I guess she must have seen something in me because she called me up out of the clear blue one day and asked me to come to work for her. So while still in high school I started on my path to learning this wonderful art. In the years since I have become known for my unique approach to the use of glass as an artists medium.

I consider myself an average, ordinary guy that is just trying to follow his dream by doing something that he loves so very much. Somehow I have been given this gift and ability to "visualize" and create. As most other artist's will tell you, I am my own worst critic.

My goal with this series of books is to not only create a nice collection of suncatcher patterns for the hobbyist but to also help address a long standing issue I have seen in this industry/hobby, which is one of confusion in regards to copyright issues for those that wish to use patterns that are available to actually make some money doing something that they really love. Each pattern has a "use license" attached to it for you.

Not everyone feels "creative" in that they can just sit down and sketch out a pattern, no matter how simple. But once they have a pattern in hand they can be extremely creative, letting their imagination take over and point them in directions they never knew existed within them.

Couple that with an "entrepreneurial" spirit and all of a sudden you have the begging's of someone that wants to start making some money doing their craft, their hobby, their art.

The only way manufacturers, wholesalers and retailers stay in business is if there is sufficient demand for the products that they sell. "Mom and Pop" type shops are what this country is built on and how communities flourish, the more we have the better our local economies are, that is a fact I fully believe in.

In this book I have taken the time to share with you my suggested retail pricing for each of the patterns that are included, some of the patterns will have more than one option in the way they can be produced, when that is the case it will be outlined on the page and the retail pricing suggestion differences will also be discussed.

This pricing is based off of either what I am actually selling these suncatchers for myself, at craft fairs, in retail settings, online etc... or based off of my nearly three decades of experience is telling me they will sell for in a general market.

With that said, you have to adjust to your particular market. If your market will sustain a higher price then you should ask a higher price, or perhaps you need to adjust just slightly down, though I would be very cautious of doing that as the suggested pricing contained in these pages are very fair. If anything, I would suggest having the occasional "sale" price, as it is far easier to lower a price than it is to raise a price.

Another consideration is mass production. I strongly suggest that when you are making these for resale you do not do so in 1 or 2 increments, you take the time and make them 6 to 12 at a time. Use up scrap glass. "Maximize" your efficiency, if you do that you maximize your return and your profits.

Here is an example. Instead of using paper for my templates on these patterns I will cut a "master pattern" out of clear picture frame glass, the thin stuff. I will make sure it is cut perfectly to the pattern, adjusted for the copper foil, ground down and so on... Then I will put small felt dots on either side of the glass, so that when I am going to place it on top of the glass I want to mark it will not scratch it. Then I will use a marker and mark around that as my pattern piece, when not using those templates I just store them in a plastic storage bag.

So lets say I have a Rose I want to make 12 of for an upcoming show. I will mark out all the glass, cut it all, grind what I need to, foil it all, assemble, solder, clean/patina/wax and am done with all 12. Versus 1 at a time. On top of that I made sure to use up some scrap I had laying around the studio.

By doing it this way I was able to make more money and keep my price down on my finished product so I could sell more. Make sense?

I have made sure to include popular patterns in this book that are good sellers for me and strike a good balance across a broad range of potential client interests, they also have proven price points that I know I can make efficiently and turn a good profit on at any given moment and am confident you can as well.

For those of you trying to sell suncatchers at various selling events my biggest advice would be to try and have a good selection of ones in the $25 to $40 range, which you will find many in this book in that range. That price range will be some of your best and most frequent sellers.

When you are making 12 of one pattern change up the color combinations so that you can appeal to a broad range of clientele.

OTHER BOOKS AVAILABLE

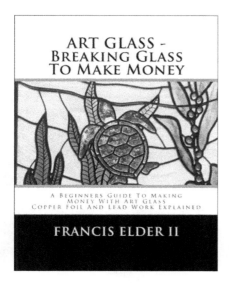

Art Glass - Breaking Glass To Make Money

A Beginners Guide To Making Money With Art Glass
Copper Foil And Lead Work Explained

List Price: $19.95
ISBN-13:   978-1536858037
ISBN-10: 153685803X

This book encompasses knowledge by the professional glass artist Francis Elder II, who has been doing stained glass and art glass work since 1988.

In this book he explains in easy to understand terms the process of going from a part time hobbyist to becoming a paid artisan. This how-to book explains in detail the steps involved that will allow you to follow your dreams of becoming a paid art glass artist.

He details areas such as; incorporating yourself into your art, designs and pattern making, efficiency, production, custom work, safety, how to price your work, installation and service calls, where and how to sell, insurance, commission sales, using social media, marketing as a whole, teaching and more.

A detailed table of contents and information on how to order autographed copies of this book can be found by visiting: http://www.booksbyelder.com/books/art-glass-breaking-glass-to-make-money-vol1/

This book is also available through various online retailers, brick and mortar book stores and big box retail stores across the country. Stained glass retailers can also order wholesale copies from me directly.

---- Dashed line represents copper wire. Create your hanging loop with a solid piece of wire that will run down the back side of the suncatcher and attach at the bottom of the suncatcher. This will create a very strong hanging loop.

Pattern: SC17071801
SG Vampz
Suggested Retail: $25.00

**CREATIONS BY ELDER
SUGGESTED GLASS**

oceanside
GLASS & TILE

spectrum
GLASS

System
96

UROBOROS
GLASS

WWW.GLASSTILE.COM

--- Dashed lines represent placement of middle fingers which are an overlay. Solder at each connecting point on front and back.

Pattern: SC17071802
SG I Love Youz
Suggested Retail: $25.00

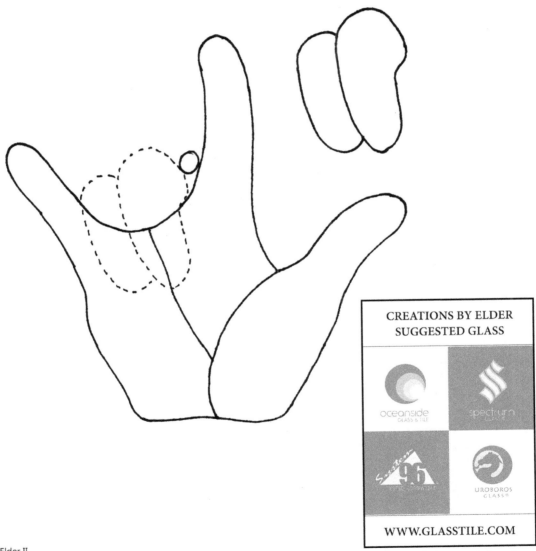

CREATIONS BY ELDER
SUGGESTED GLASS

WWW.GLASSTILE.COM

CreationsByElder.com

--- Dashed lines represent wire.

1. The spout has the center part of it made from one solid piece of wire that goes from the top curly part along the backside of the whale to the bottom and attaches at the bottom, this strengthens the "hanging loop" which is the top curly part of this. Then you can add additional curly parts to create the water spout of the whale.

2. This is another wire overlay that forms the mouth of the whale, creating a smile and then you attach the eye to the end of that smile. I like to use glass nuggets for the eyes.

3. Sometimes I will turn the fins of the tail upwards a little, giving the suncatcher a little bit of a 3 dimensional effect.

Pattern: SC17071803
SG Whalez
Suggested Retail: $20.00

CREATIONS BY ELDER
SUGGESTED GLASS

oceanside

spectrum

UROBOROS GLASS

WWW.GLASSTILE.COM

--- Dashed lines represent copper wire. One solid piece of wire attaches from base of beak through tail and attaches to base of tail (on the backside of the bird), this helps stabilize the tail. Another piece of wire forms one of the curly cues on the birds head and then runs along the body in between the body and the beak to the base of the body with another piece of wire attached to form the feet this would normally be the one next to the #2 as the bird will hang from that curly cue most of the time.

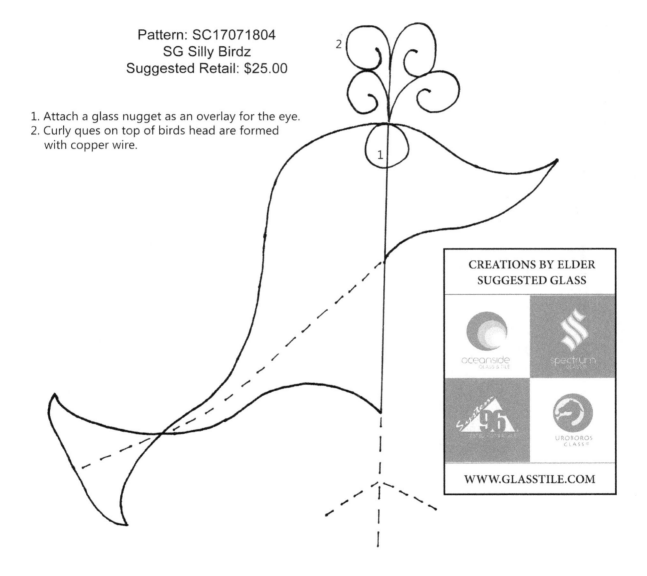

Pattern: SC17071804
SG Silly Birdz
Suggested Retail: $25.00

1. Attach a glass nugget as an overlay for the eye.
2. Curly ques on top of birds head are formed with copper wire.

**CREATIONS BY ELDER
SUGGESTED GLASS**

oceanside
GLASS & TILE

spectrum
GLASS

S96
TESTED COMPATIBLE

UROBOROS
GLASS

WWW.GLASSTILE.COM

--- Hanging loop should be made out of a longer piece of wire that will follow the curved line down, as an overlay to the copper foil, to the center nugget and then be soldered into place. Using a smaller gauge wire, like an 18 gauge will allow you to build up the solder line like normal so that the wire is hidden. This will integrate the loop making it very strong. Attaching the wire on the backside will hide any "hump" in the solder line.

1. When making this pattern I cut out the halves of the yin yang as solid and then use a 3/4" grinder head to remove the center hole. Then I put a glass nugget in the center hole. This really looks nice and adds a lot of sparkle. You could also use a faceted gem or cut a piece of art glass.

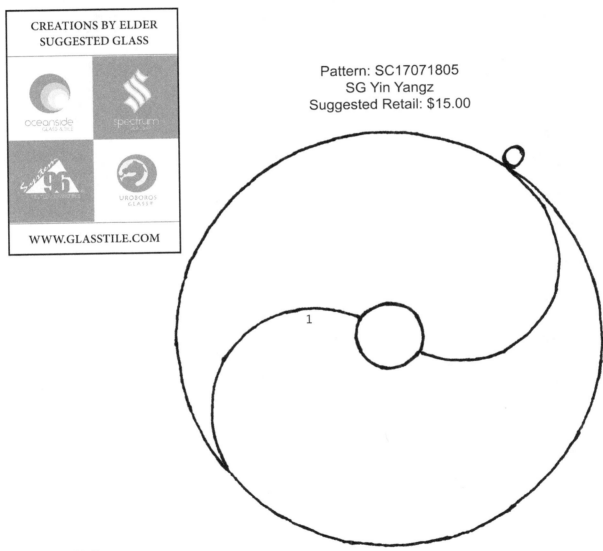

**CREATIONS BY ELDER
SUGGESTED GLASS**

oceanside
GLASS & TILE

spectrum
GLASS

96
TESTED COMPATIBLE

UROBOROS
GLASS

WWW.GLASSTILE.COM

Pattern: SC17071805
SG Yin Yangz
Suggested Retail: $15.00

1

--- Dashed line represents copper wire. Create a hanging loop with solid wire that runs along the backside of the flower to the base of the stem, soldered at each point of contact. Creating a very strong loop and reinforcing the stem.

Pattern: SC17071806
SG Calla Lilliez
Suggested Retail: $25.00

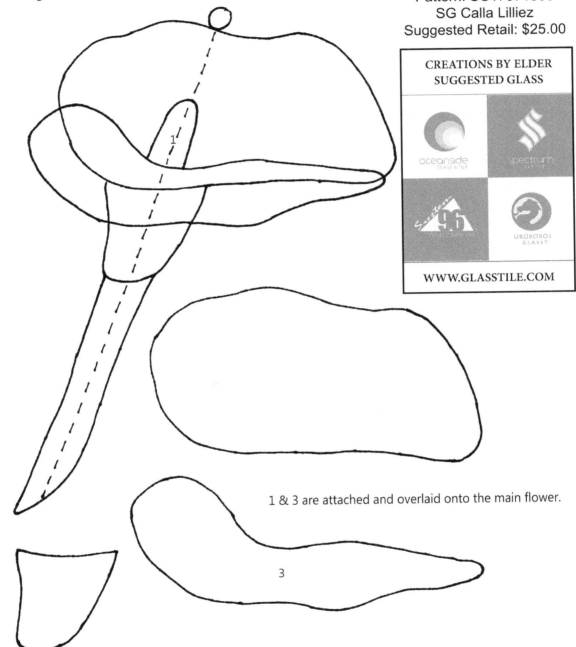

CREATIONS BY ELDER
SUGGESTED GLASS

WWW.GLASSTILE.COM

1 & 3 are attached and overlaid onto the main flower.

There can be two options for the production of this suncatcher. The lines that break up the interior of the pumpkin can either be individual pieces of glass (Option A) or the lines can be overlays of copper wire over one solid piece of glass (Option B).

Pattern: SC17071807
SG Pumpkinz
Suggested Retail: Option A $30.00 or Option A $18.00

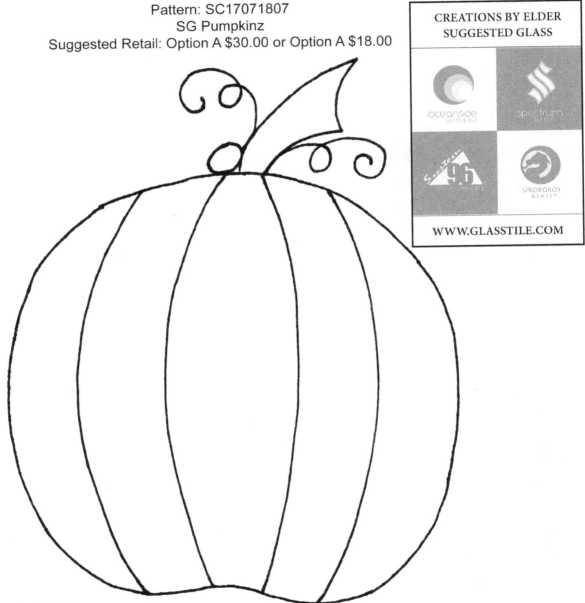

CREATIONS BY ELDER
SUGGESTED GLASS

oceanside
GLASS & TILE

spectrum
GLASS

System 96
GLASSES COMPATIBLE

UROBOROS
GLASS©

WWW.GLASSTILE.COM

Petals (2) of the tropical flower are overlaid over the leaves (1), this gives a nice 3 dimensional feel. The center of the flower (3) can be a glass nugget or faceted jewel. When you build this piece you will want to build the petals (2) and the center of the flower (3) as one flat piece, then the leaves will attach at the backside around the center of the flower. In addition, if you want to make this to be a piece that sits on a table instead of a hanging suncatcher, you can instead angle the leaves (1) down to act as "feet" to support the flower. See next page for individual petal and flower patterns.

CREATIONS BY ELDER
SUGGESTED GLASS

oceanside
GLASS & TILE

spectrum
GLASS

System 96
FUSED COMPATIBLE

UROBOROS
GLASS®

WWW.GLASSTILE.COM

Pattern: SC17071808A
SG Tropical Flowerz
Suggested Retail: $55.00

2

1

3

CreationsByElder.com

Pattern: SC17071808B
SG Tropical Flowerz
Suggested Retail: $55.00

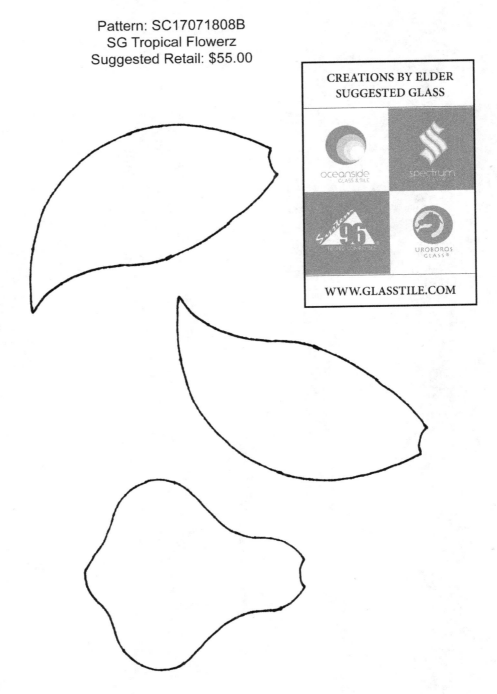

CreationsByElder.com

--- Dashed lines represent copper wire.

Pattern: SC17071809
SG Rosez
Suggested Retail: $55.00

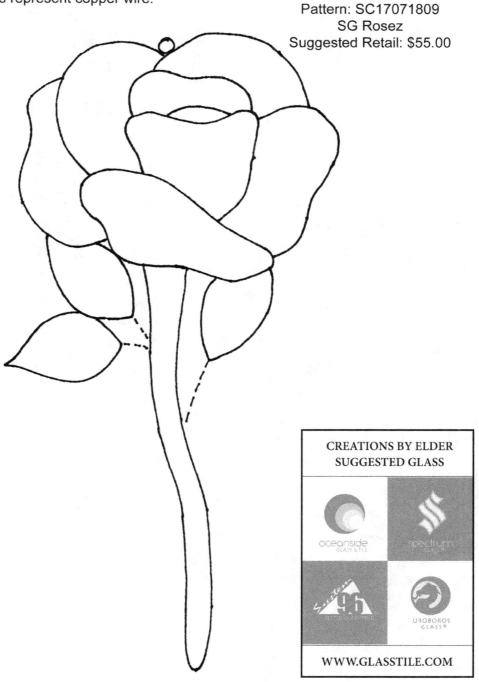

--- Dashed line represents copper wire that overlays and attaches on top of suncatcher and continues on to form the "beak" of the hummingbird. The eye is a glob of solder.

Pattern: SC17071810
SG Hummingbyrdz
Suggested Retail: $25.00

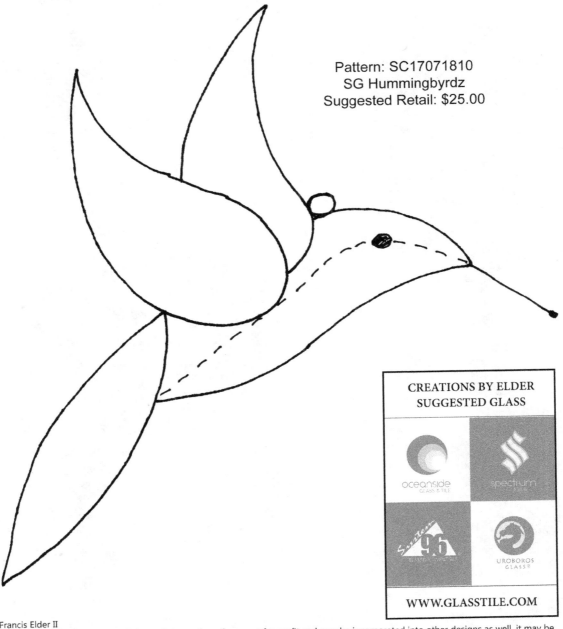

CREATIONS BY ELDER
SUGGESTED GLASS

oceanside
GLASS & TILE

spectrum
GLASS

System
9.6
GLASS COMPATIBLE

UROBOROS
GLASS

WWW.GLASSTILE.COM

Pattern: SC17071811
SG Hummingbirdz
Suggested Retail: $30.00

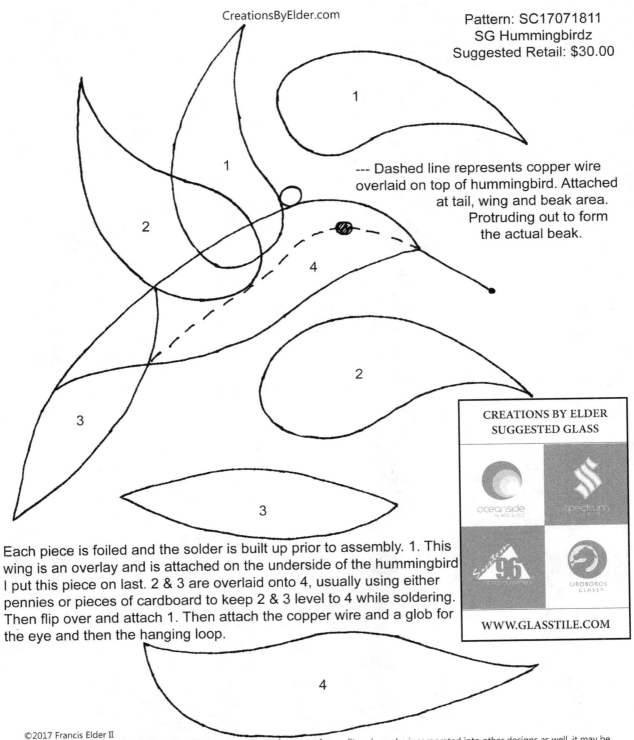

1

1

2

--- Dashed line represents copper wire overlaid on top of hummingbird. Attached at tail, wing and beak area. Protruding out to form the actual beak.

4

2

3

3

CREATIONS BY ELDER
SUGGESTED GLASS

oceanside
GLASS & TILE

spectrum
GLASS

System 96

UROBOROS
GLASS

WWW.GLASSTILE.COM

Each piece is foiled and the solder is built up prior to assembly. 1. This wing is an overlay and is attached on the underside of the hummingbird. I put this piece on last. 2 & 3 are overlaid onto 4, usually using either pennies or pieces of cardboard to keep 2 & 3 level to 4 while soldering. Then flip over and attach 1. Then attach the copper wire and a glob for the eye and then the hanging loop.

4

--- Dashed lines represent copper wire. Bend one solid piece to form each foot with a "U" shape that will attach at the base of the bird. Then attach two small sections to form each foot. The eye is a solder glob. (1) Represents where you will want to attach a piece of thin gauge wire to reinforce the tail.

Pattern: SC17071812
SG Red Birdz
Suggested Retail: $40.00

1

CREATIONS BY ELDER
SUGGESTED GLASS

oceanside

spectrum

System 96

UROBOROS GLASS

WWW.GLASSTILE.COM

--- Needles are attached "V" shaped pieces of copper wire and they can be "pointed" out from the cactus to give a 3 dimensional feel.

Pattern: SC17071813
SG CACTUZ
Suggested Retail: $20.00

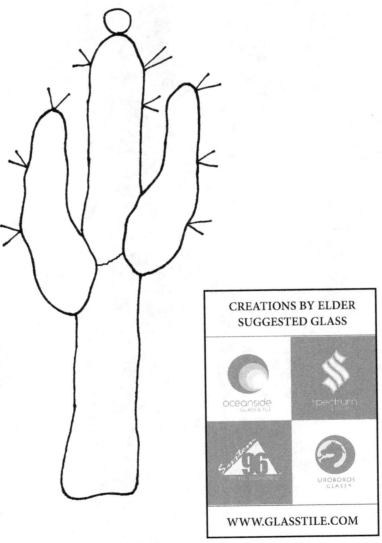

CREATIONS BY ELDER
SUGGESTED GLASS

WWW.GLASSTILE.COM

--- This suncatcher can be made one of three ways. The center line (A) can either be option 1 where it represents a copper wire overlay on a solid piece of glass that makes up the skull, so the skull is one piece of glass plus the horns. Or the skull is three pieces of glass, plus the horns, option 2. Both of these options are shown with the skull being attached to a ring (B) which you can either buy or create from solid copper wire. The "hanging loop" is shown but not really required, as the piece can be hung from the actual metal ring. Option 3 is where you cut glass to fill the background areas. You can "drop" these into the ring itself, so that the skull has an overlay effect, you will want to use some pennies or cardboard to support the skull while you solder up the joint that connects the background to the skull. This will give the piece a 3 dimensional feel. The hanging loop will then need to be utilized. Make sure it is solidly connected.

Pattern: SC17071814
SG SOUTHWEST SKULLZ
Suggested Retail: Option 1. $25.00   Option 2. $35.00   Option 3 $45.00

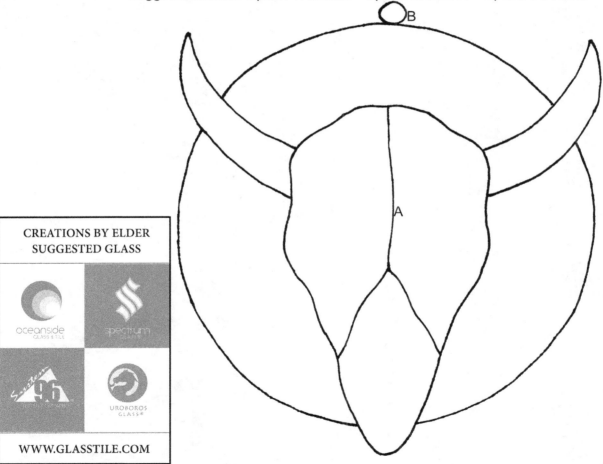

CREATIONS BY ELDER
SUGGESTED GLASS

oceanside
GLASS & TILE

spectrum

96

UROBOROS
GLASS®

WWW.GLASSTILE.COM

--- This suncatcher can be made with two options. Option 1 would be where the top fin and tail fin are solid pieces of glass and the lines you see are actually overlaid pieces of copper wire. In this case, "A" represents a hanging loop that is a solid piece of copper wire that goes from the top of the top fin, overlaid across the body and down through the ventral fin (middle bottom). Option 2 is where each fin is an individual piece of glass and the hanging loop is a solid piece of copper wire that follows the same path as outlined before. This creates a nicely reinforced hanging loop. The body in both options is a solid piece of glass. The eye is an overlaid glass nugget.

**CREATIONS BY ELDER
SUGGESTED GLASS**

oceanside
GLASS & TILE

spectrum
GLASS

System 96
TESTED COMPATIBLE

UROBOROS
GLASS®

WWW.GLASSTILE.COM

Pattern: SC17071815
SG FISHIEZ
Suggested Retail: Option 1 $25.00 Option 2 $40.00

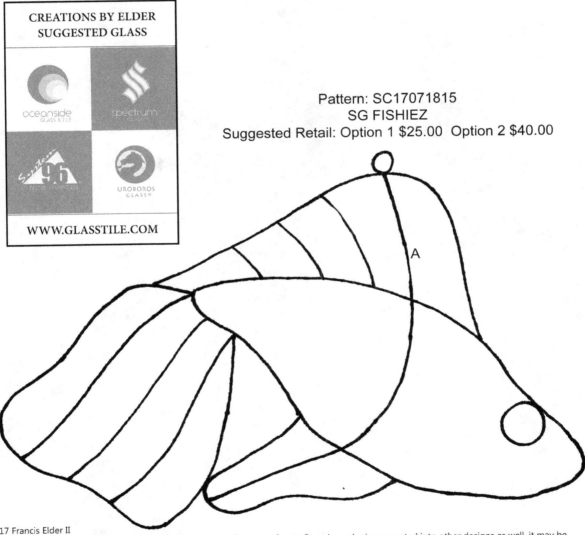

A

--- Dashed line represents copper wire. Create a hanging loop that is solid wire that attaches on the back from the top of the head to the bottom of the turtle, soldered at each point it contacts. This will create a reinforced hanging loop. The eyes are overlaid glass nuggets.

Pattern: SC17071816
SG SEA TURTLEZ
Suggested Retail: $30.00

CREATIONS BY ELDER
SUGGESTED GLASS

oceanside
GLASS & TILE

spectrum
GLASS

96
System 96

UROBOROS
GLASS®

WWW.GLASSTILE.COM

--- Dashed line represents copper wire. Create the hanging loop out of a solid piece of copper wire that extends down the back of the lizard and down to the base of the skull, attaching at each point of contact. This creates a reinforced hanging loop. Feet can be glass nuggets. You can also make the skull of the lizard into one solid piece and make the eyes out of overlaid glass nuggets.

Pattern: SC17071817
SG LIZARDZ
Suggested Retail: $55.00

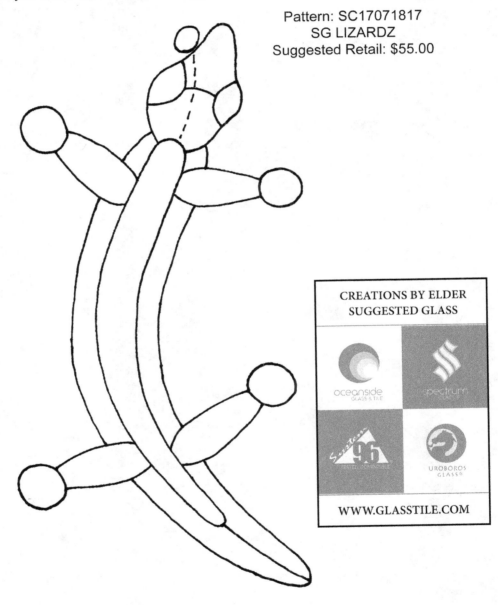

CREATIONS BY ELDER
SUGGESTED GLASS

WWW.GLASSTILE.COM

--- The eye of this Hummy Birdz is a solder glob and the beak is a piece of solid copper wire.

Pattern: SC17071818
SG HUMMY BIRDZ
Suggested Retail: $55.00

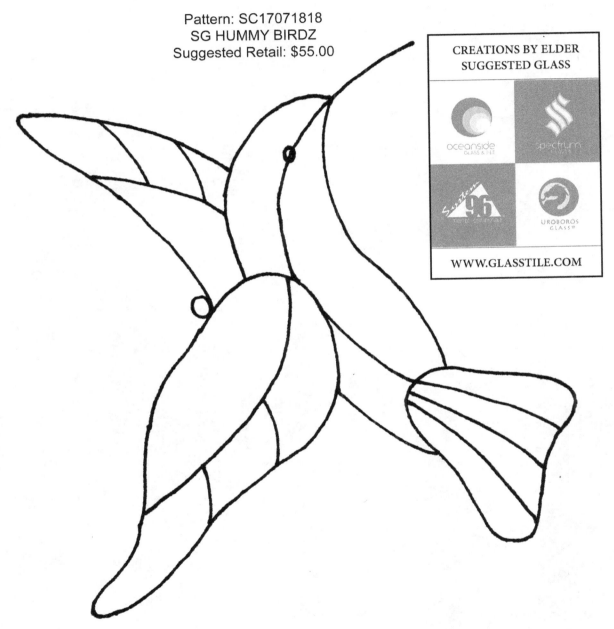

CREATIONS BY ELDER
SUGGESTED GLASS

oceanside
GLASS & TILE

spectrum
GLASS

96

UROBOROS
GLASS

WWW.GLASSTILE.COM

--- Dashed lines represent copper wire. This wire is attached at the back of the "pot" for the Bonsai Treez and each of the "bushy" parts of the tree. The hanging loop is one solid piece that travels down to the base of the "pot", this creates a very strong integrated hanging loop. Each of the "limbs" that travel down and through the lowest bushy part are attached to the backside of that bushy part. This gives strength and rigidity to the upper limbs.

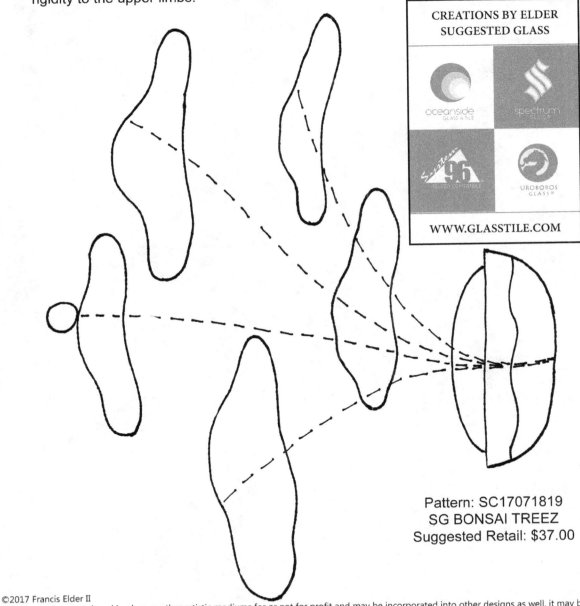

CREATIONS BY ELDER
SUGGESTED GLASS

oceanside
GLASS & TILE

spectrum
GLASS

9.6
TESTED COMPATIBLE

UROBOROS
GLASS®

WWW.GLASSTILE.COM

Pattern: SC17071819
SG BONSAI TREEZ
Suggested Retail: $37.00

--- Dashed line represents solid copper wire which is the actual hanging loop and goes from top to bottom of the Dragonfliez, this creates a very strong hanging loop and also strengthens the body. Looking at figure (A) you will see an outline showing how the wire loop starts at the head of the Dragonfliez, under the head, then bends up and between the head and body to go along the top of the body. The wings then can be attached to the body and touch at the wire in the middle. If you want you can also angle the wings up from the body to give them a 3 dimensional effect. The head can be a glass nugget.

Pattern: SC17071820
SG Dragonfliez
Suggested Retail: Option 1. $35.00
Option 2. $45.00 Option 3. $55.00

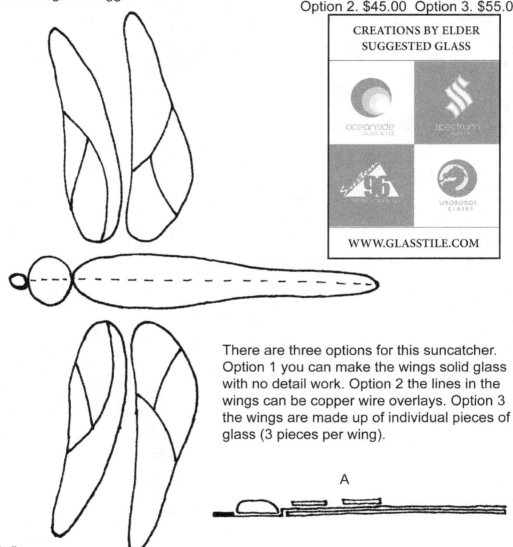

CREATIONS BY ELDER
SUGGESTED GLASS

oceanside
GLASS & TILE

spectrum

96

UROBOROS
GLASS

WWW.GLASSTILE.COM

There are three options for this suncatcher. Option 1 you can make the wings solid glass with no detail work. Option 2 the lines in the wings can be copper wire overlays. Option 3 the wings are made up of individual pieces of glass (3 pieces per wing).

A

--- There are a couple of options for the production of these SG Featherz. Option 1 the detail work on the inside of the feather can either be an overlay of solid copper wire on a solid piece of glass, if you go this route the hanging loop should be one solid piece that then travels from the top of the feather to the base of the feather, this will create a reinforced hanging loop. Then the rest of the details are pieces of copper wire that attach to that center piece and outwards to the edge of the feather. Option 2 is where the detail work of the feather are individual pieces of glass. Going with this option you could use a thinner gauge copper wire to do a solid hanging loop and wire that goes from the top of the feather to the base that will also create a very strong hanging loop.

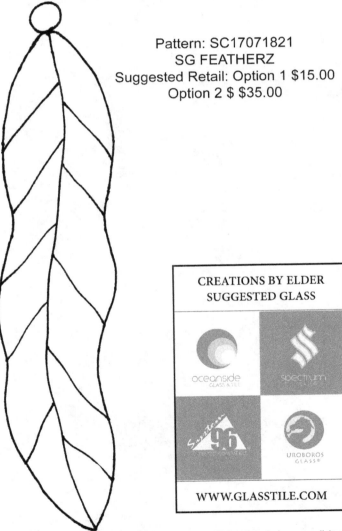

Pattern: SC17071821
SG FEATHERZ
Suggested Retail: Option 1 $15.00
Option 2 $ $35.00

CREATIONS BY ELDER
SUGGESTED GLASS

oceanside
GLASS & TILE

spectrum

96
System

UROBOROS
GLASS®

WWW.GLASSTILE.COM

--- This is another "layered" suncatcher. The nose (3) and one of the eyes (1) are an overlay of the face and attached at the end of the nose at the face and the smile (A) which is a piece of copper wire with the other eye (1) attached to the end as an overlay as well which is attached at the bottom of the face. Figure B is the hanging loop which is a solid piece of wire that is connected along the back of the suncatcher from the top of the suncatcher to the base of the suncatcher, this creates a very solid integrated hanging loop. Number 1 and 2 can be a glass nuggets.

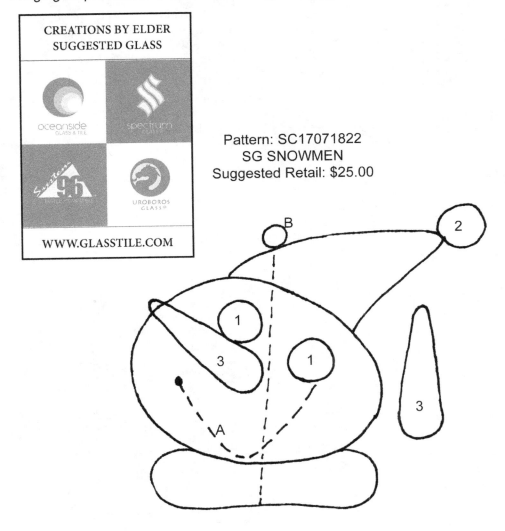

CREATIONS BY ELDER
SUGGESTED GLASS

oceanside
GLASS & TILE

spectrum
GLASS

9.6

UROBOROS
GLASS

WWW.GLASSTILE.COM

Pattern: SC17071822
SG SNOWMEN
Suggested Retail: $25.00

--- Dashed line represents solid copper wire. This is a free standing piece. The windows (A) are overlaid onto the roof and main part of the house. The detail work of the windows (B) are solid copper wire overlays. To strengthen the house you will want to wrap the entire house in solid copper wire, extending the wire down to form the legs (C). You can use a thicker gauge wire for the feet of the legs or even a piece of U zinc. You might even want to instead of creating feet use a piece of wood and drill two holes that the legs can slid down into, creating a base for the piece. Then you could glue some glass nuggets to the wood and create a "path" to the house.

Pattern: SC17071823
SG SPOOKY HOUZE
Suggested Retail: $30.00

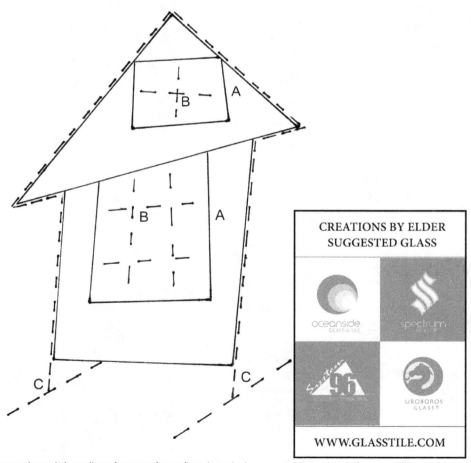

--- Dashed line represents solid copper wire hanging loop that then goes down along the backside of the Christmas Ornamentz to attach in the middle. This helps to strengthen the piece and the make a strong integrated hanging loop.

Pattern: SC17071824
SG CHRISTMAS ORNAMENTZ 1
Suggested Retail: $25.00

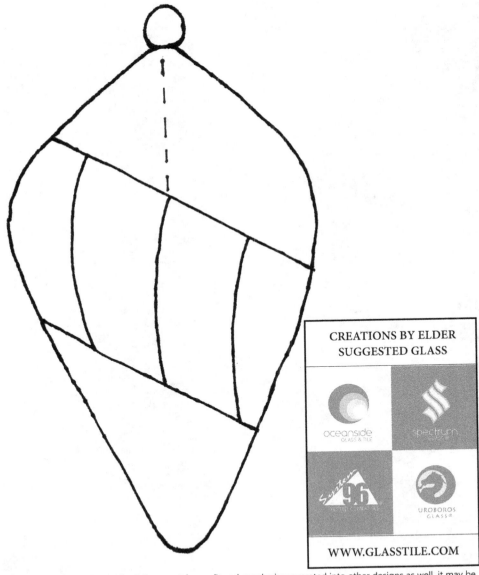

CREATIONS BY ELDER
SUGGESTED GLASS

oceanside
GLASS & TILE

spectrum

System 96

UROBOROS
GLASS

WWW.GLASSTILE.COM

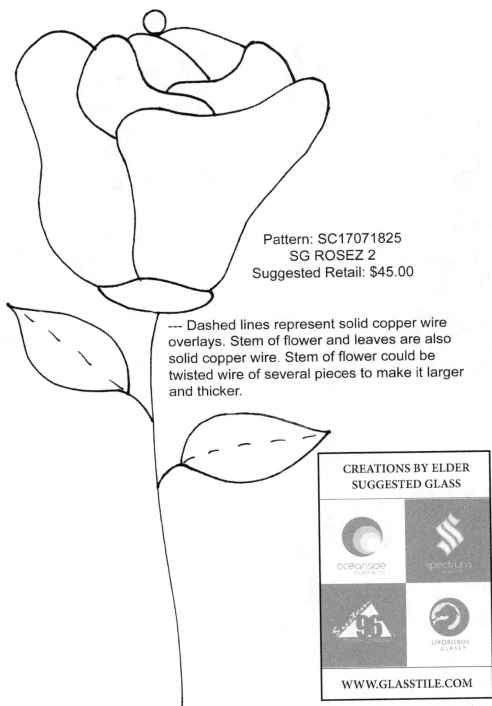

Pattern: SC17071825
SG ROSEZ 2
Suggested Retail: $45.00

--- Dashed lines represent solid copper wire overlays. Stem of flower and leaves are also solid copper wire. Stem of flower could be twisted wire of several pieces to make it larger and thicker.

CREATIONS BY ELDER SUGGESTED GLASS

oceanside
GLASS & TILE

spectrum
GLASS

System
96
TESTED COMPATIBLE

UROBOROS
GLASS

WWW.GLASSTILE.COM

Special Acknowledgement

I would like to take a moment and give a special thank you to Oceanside Glass & Tile in Carlsbad, California, who helped sponsor this book and are continuing the lines of Spectrum and Uroboros art glass. I hope each of you will take a moment and stop by their website to check out the current news about those art glass product lines and the selections currently available: www.glasstile.com

I would also like to take a moment and give credit to one of my youngest sons, Ethan, for the suncatchers that are featured on this book, as he made the ones that are pictured. Not only showing talent and ability at a young age but also a desire to create "quality" always made me proud, I hope that he continues on his path of creativity and self expression. While we were at craft shows he would get such a sense of fulfillment when someone purchased one of his pieces, especially when they stated how much they loved them. It would put a smile on his face that would go from ear to ear.

One last story I would like to share with you my reader, as a proud papa, is a time when another vendors child had come to our booth and had been bragging about how many expensive phones he had broken on purpose because he was frustrated with them. Only to have his mother and father replace them, over and over again. Ethan, probably only a year or so older, looked at this young man and told him something like this; "Well, I would never do that. Because I earn my money. I value what I buy.".

Now that folks was one of the proudest moments in my life!

CPSIA information can be obtained
at www.ICGtesting.com
Printed in the USA
BVHW021649250523
664889BV00009B/366

9 781973 794899